A SIP OF AESOP

by **JANE YOLEN**

illustrated by **Karen Barbour**

THE BLUE SKY PRESS

An Imprint of Scholastic Inc. • New York

For my new granddaughter, Maddison Jane
— J. Y.

For Jasper and Lucy
— K. B.

THE BLUE SKY PRESS

Text copyright © 1995 by Jane Yolen
Illustrations copyright © 1995 by Karen Barbour

For information regarding permission, please write to:
Permissions Department,
The Blue Sky Press, an imprint of Scholastic Inc.,
555 Broadway, New York, New York 10012.
The Blue Sky Press is a registered trademark of Scholastic Inc.

Library of Congress Cataloging-in-Publication Data
Yolen, Jane.
A sip of Aesop / by Jane Yolen; illustrations by Karen Barbour.
p.   cm.
Summary: Retells, in verse, thirteen fables from the Greek
slave, Aesop, including "The Hare and the Tortoise," "The Boy
Who Cried Wolf," and "The Fox and the Stork."
ISBN 0-590-47895-8
1. Aesop's fables—Adaptations.   [1. Fables.   2. Stories in
rhyme.]   I. Aesop.   II. Barbour, Karen, ill.   III. Title.
PZ8.3.Y76Si   1995   811'.54—dc20
94-41002   CIP   AC

12 11 10 9 8 7 6 5 4 3 2 1   5 6 7 8 9/9 0/0
Printed in the United States of America   37
First printing, September 1995

Production supervision by Angela Biola
Designed by Kathleen Westray

CONTENTS

WHY AESOP?

Aesop was an ancient Greek
And spoke no language I can speak.
So I have put his tales in verse
With hopes I haven't made them worse.

MORAL:
In prose or rhyme
There is a moral:
Aesop Aeppeals
In print — or oral.

THE HARE AND THE TORTOISE

"Slowpoke, lowpoke,"
Called the hare.
"You no-go-poke
Anywhere."

Tortoise answered,
"Slow as day,
I'll outrun you
Anyway."

An oval racetrack
They laid out
To prove the faster
Without doubt.

Out in front
Hare quickly leapt,
While steady, steady
Tortoise crept.

Then halfway there,
Hare took a nap,
So tortoise caught him
On that lap.

Hare dreamed his winnings
Quite away,
And tortoise took
The prize that day.

MORAL:
If naps and laps
You do confuse,
Then you are surely
Bound to lose.

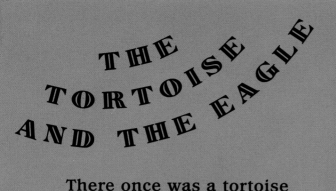

THE TORTOISE AND THE EAGLE

There once was a tortoise
Who wanted to fly
And begged a proud eagle
To carry him high.

So winningly Tortoise
Did argue his cause,
The eagle ascended
With him in its claws.

Then over the mountaintop
Proud Eagle flew
With Tortoise as co-pilot,
Wingman, and crew.

"Now drop me," said Tortoise,
"And watch how I fly."
He spread out his legs —
And fell from the sky.

MORAL:
Demand what you can't do,
Demand your own ruin.
So do what you can,
Or yourself you will do in.

THE DOG AND THE BONE

Crossing a bridge
With a bone in his teeth,
A dog stopped to stare
At the river beneath.

And what did he see
In that watery shine?
"There's a dog right below
With a bone just like mine.

"If I could get *that* bone,
Then I would have two,
A much nicer number
On which I can chew."

He snatched for that second,
But opening his mouth,
His barks all flew northward,
His bone — it went south.

It splashed in the river,
Quite dousing Our Hero,
And sunk. So he slunk home,
A bone count of zero.

MORAL:
You may not have time
For a final correction.
Don't open your mouth
Without proper reflection.

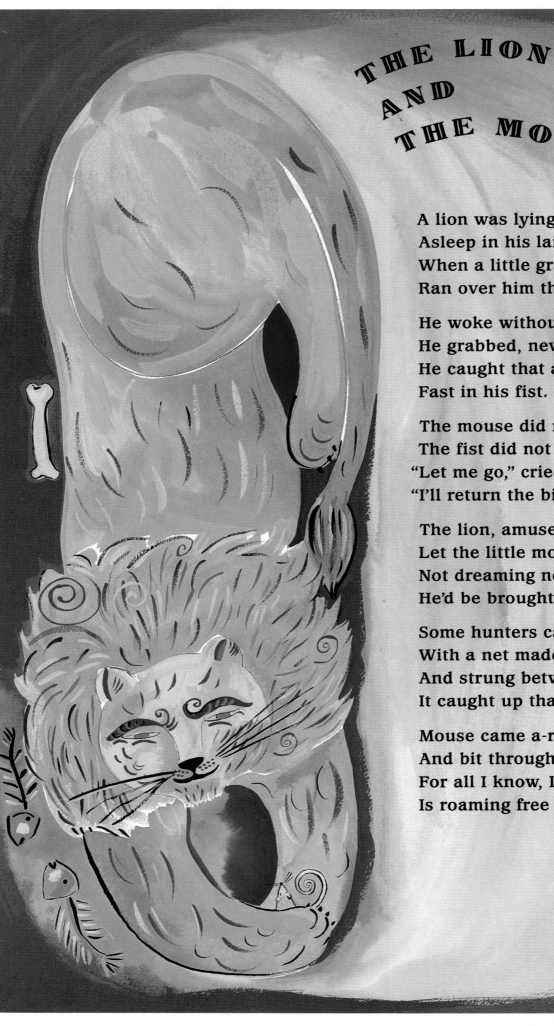

THE LION AND THE MOUSE

A lion was lying
Asleep in his lair
When a little gray mouse
Ran over him there.

He woke without thinking;
He grabbed, never missed.
He caught that adventurer
Fast in his fist.

The mouse did not struggle;
The fist did not waver.
"Let me go," cried the mouse.
"I'll return the big favor."

The lion, amused,
Let the little mouse go,
Not dreaming next day
He'd be brought mighty low.

Some hunters came by
With a net made of nylon,
And strung between trees,
It caught up that proud li-on.

Mouse came a-running
And bit through the net.
For all I know, Lion
Is roaming free yet.

MORAL:
Belittle your friends,
You'll have none you can call;
But little friends can prove
The greatest of all.

THE FOX AND THE GRAPES

In a vineyard
High on the vine,
Hung juicy grapes
All in a line.

"Those grapes look swell!"
The fox declared,
"Especially since
They won't be shared.

"They're sweet and ripe
And oh-so-fine,
And best of all,
Those grapes are mine!"

He jumped and jumped
Till he grew thinner,
But could not reach
One grape for dinner.

He slunk away,
His stomach shrunk,
Now sure each grape
Was old — and stunk.

"Those grapes are
Under-ripe," he said.
"Before I eat one,
I'll be dead."

MORAL:
High or low
Upon the vine,
Sour grapes
Make an awful whine.

THE FOX AND THE CROW

A crow once found
A piece of cheese
And flew into
A copse of trees.

Below, a hungry
Fox looked up
And on that cheddar
Longed to sup.

"Oh Crow," quoth Fox,
"You are so rare,
A beauty quite
Beyond compare.

"Your voice must be
A treasure, too.
The Queen of Birds,
By gosh — it's you!

"Sing me a song,
Rock, jazz, or blues,
Or any other
Form you choose."

The crow, quite flattered,
Tried to croon
Her favorite song,
A top-ten tune.

She opened wide;
Out dropped the cheddar.
The fox had never
Tasted better.

M O R A L :
Cheddar, Edam,
Swiss, or Brie —
It's oil the same
In flattery.

THE GRASSHOPPER AND THE ANTS

The grasshopper fiddled
The whole summer long.
He filled the green fields
With his bright, silly song.

The ants, on the other hand,
Worked up a sweat,
Putting away
All the goods they could get.

When wintertime came,
The poor hopper was famished,
For all of his food
Had entirely vanished.

"Please feed me!" he begged,
"Or — alas — I will die."
"Go lunch on your fiddle,"
The ants did reply.

MORAL:
Whether a star
Or a low second-rater,
Only play now
And you'll have to pay later.

THE MICE IN COUNCIL

The mice called a meeting
At which they all sat
Discussing the way
To get rid of their cat.

"Poison!" one cried.
(A real silly suggestion.)
Hanging and shooting
Were out of the question.

At last they agreed
That the mice would bedeck
Their menace by placing
A bell round his neck.

That way they could hear
When he went on a stroll.
"We'll make an invincible
Feline patrol."

"Good plan," said one old mouse,
A fine diplomat.
"But answer me — *who* will go
Bell that mean cat?"

MORAL:
To make a good plan
Is but half a solution.
How close are the words
Execute — execution.

THE FROG AND THE OX

In a muddy pond
Beside a bog
There lived a tadpole
And a frog.

The tad was tiny,
Frog was not.
(Though he was smaller
Than he thought!)

One day an ox
Grazed by the bog.
"Oh, what a giant!"
Cried Wee Frog.

The big frog preened,
"I'm just his size,"
But saw denial
In Tad's eyes.

Frog puffed and puffed
His froggy figger
Until he grew
A small bit bigger.

"Am I as big?"
Big Frog inquired,
Wanting to be
The most admired.

"Not big enough,"
Admitted Tad.
This statement made
The big frog mad.

Puff — puff — puff — puff —
He tried his worst.
And then with one more puff —
He burst.

MORAL:
You may never be
As big as you think.
Some need a shrinking,
And some need a shrink.

THE BOY WHO CRIED WOLF

A shepherd boy
Once got his kicks
By on his neighbors
Playing tricks.

"A wolf! A wolf!"
He cried aloud
And gathered quite
A village crowd.

The second time
He gathered more.
They came at three.
They came at four.

These tricks did anger
And annoy
The neighbors of
The shepherd boy.

And when he tried
To call at six,
They said: "We *won't* fall
For your tricks."

No sooner had he
Lost their ear
Than who but real wolves
Did appear.

"A wolf! A wolf!"
He cried in vain.
Soon every sheep
He had was slain.

MORAL:
Cry wolf once,
You'll be believed.
Cry wolf lots,
And you'll be grieved.

Stork and Fox
Were once good friends
Till food served but
The means to ends.

"Please come to dinner,
Mrs. Stork.
We will not need
A knife or fork.

"Come right at eight.
Ring twice, three knocks."
Signed — "Your best friend,
Mr. Fox."

But all Fox served
To Stork at eight
Was meatless soup
On a broad, flat plate,

Which he could slurp,
But she could not.
(He hadn't given
This much thought.)

When Fox came by
Next day for tea,
Stork turned the tables
Artfully.

She served the food
In a long-necked jar.
At eating, Fox
Could not get far.

And so food served
To make them foes;
A tasty moral,
I suppose.

MORAL:
Do it first
For your own fun,
And next you will
Yourself be done.

THE DOG IN THE MANGER

Dogs eat meat
And donkeys hay.
That is just
Old Nature's way.

Now Dog one day
Was left alone
Without so much
As a well-gnawed bone.

But Donkey had
A manger high
With ripened hay
And wheat and rye.

So Dog leaped up
Upon the hay
And barked to keep
The ass away.

Dog growled and howled,
He gnashed his teeth,
And spit upon
The hay beneath.

"Since I do not have
Any meat,"
He said, "I shall not
Let *you* eat."

Eventually
They both grew thinner
And died from never
Eating dinner.

MORAL:
Just because
It's not *your* taste,
Don't let a good meal
Go to waste.

COUNTING
YOUR CHICKENS

From market, from market
The farm girl did trot,
Counting twelve chickens
She had not yet got.

From market, from market
With one dozen eggs,
That farm girl skipped dreamily
On careless legs.

She stepped in a pothole,
She stumbled and fell,
And all of her chickens
Leaked out of the shell.

MORAL:
Girl and chicks
Were quite a match.
Eggs and dreams
Take time to hatch.

ABOUT AESOP

THERE IS VERY LITTLE that we really know about Aesop. He was a slave most of his life, living on the Greek island of Samos early in the sixth century B.C. The rest is all guesswork. Some guesses are that he was ugly and ill-formed, that he was an advisor to the king of Lydia, that he offended people in power and was executed. But no one can be sure.

He never wrote down his *Fables* during his life, but long after his death they began to be published in many forms. The first collection attributed to Aesop was in prose. We only know about that book from other sources; no copy of the actual book has survived. Aesop in rhyme has been popular since the first century, but the most famous rhymed version was written in French by Jean de La Fontaine in the seventeenth century.

There are over two hundred fables attributed to Aesop, so a book of thirteen is a "sip" indeed.

J
811
Y

Yolen, Jane.

A sip of Aesop.

DATE